Shat Naman

Verses of Spiritual Oneness

Neha Modgil

BookLeaf Publishing

India | USA | UK

Made with ❤ on the BookLeaf Publishing Platform

www.bookleafpub.in
www.bookleafpub.com

Dedication

To my husband, my mentor and guide on this spiritual journey. Your wisdom and direction have been my compass on the path towards the Divine.

To my children, whose boundless energy resonates in harmony with the light of the Almighty, inspiring me each day.

And to my parents, who planted in me the seeds of Spirituality and Oneness. Your love has been the foundation of this path.

With deepest gratitude, I dedicate this work to you.

Acknowledgements

I would like to express my heartfelt gratitude to my children for giving me the space and time to pen down my thoughts. My deepest thanks to my parents for planting the seed of spirituality in me, which has shaped my journey. I am also grateful to my sisters for reviewing my poems and offering their valuable contributions to my writing. A special thank you to my husband for guiding me on the path of spirituality and for his unwavering support. Lastly, I would like to extend my appreciation to Google for being an invaluable resource in helping me research and delve deeper into the topics I explored in this book.

Preface

This collection of poems is a journey through the sacred and divine. It is my humble attempt to honour the many paths that lead us to a single, unifying light, to express the deep reverence and love I hold for the Divine in all its forms.

In writing these verses, I sought to celebrate not just my own faith, but the faiths of many, recognising that each name we call brings us closer to the universal truth within us all. Through these words, I hope to offer a sense of peace, gratitude and connectedness to readers from all backgrounds.

This book is inspired by the people who have guided and sustained me on my own spiritual path. My husband has been my mentor and companion in this journey, sharing his wisdom and helping me find clarity. My children, with their joyful spirits, reflect the divine energy that keeps me grounded and uplifted. And my parents, who nurtured the seed of spirituality in me, instilled in me a sense of oneness with all creation.

It is my sincere hope that these poems resonate with you, offering a moment of reflection, a spark of inspiration and a reminder of the divine connection we all share. May this collection serve as a small bridge between paths, reminding us that in each name and every faith, there is a common thread of love and light.

To the Great Ones

Ram, Guru Nanak, Jesus and Buddha–
Names we've called with love and awe.
You gave us all, you shared your grace,
    Seeing not our caste or race.

    You sat with us, blessed every soul,
        Guiding us to make us whole.
Your path of peace, your light so true,
Led us towards joy, both old and new.

    Saviours of peace, revered and pure,
To you, our hearts and hopes endure.
With endless respect, we bow to thee–
    Shat Shat Naman, eternally.

Path of Dharma

As Shri Ram took his vow,
To leave Ayodhya, renounce his crown,
To honour his father's sacred word,
And journey forth to forest ground.

Sita Mata, quick to stand,
In loyalty took his hand.
Knowing no home but by his side,
She left her comforts, opulence aside,
To walk with him through thick and thin,
Wherever fate might lead them in.

Lakshman, the brother, followed, too–
Fourteen years he journeyed through.
Protector, friend, steadfast and true,
With heart devoted, purpose clear,
In reverence, he drew near.

They taught us Dharma's timeless call:
To keep our word, to give our all.
To walk beside, through trials deep,
The ones we love, our oaths to keep.

To stand with family when they're in pain,
To hold the right, though trials remain.
To uphold truth, against all odds,
And walk the path laid out by Gods.

Good Over Evil

As Shri Ram prepared for war,
Ravana mocked, with scornful roar,
Calling him a humble seer,
Too small to conquer, too weak to fear.

Hanuman, teased and tail aflame,
Stood undeterred, true to his name.
Angad's strength dismissed and cast aside,
Yet he stood firm with fearless pride.

Yet stones began to float on sea,
Forming a bridge for the army's decree.
And Vibishan, loyal and wise,
Stood with the righteous, where truth lies.

For when we walk the path of right,
The forces of the world unite.
Evil may taunt, yet goodness prevails,
As the light of dharma never fails.

In the end, the lesson clear and strong–
Good will triumph over wrong.

Maryada Purushottam

Leaving behind kingdom, wealth and
splendour,
Shri Ram marched to the jungle, in complete
surrender.
To honour his father, his vow he upheld,
Refusing Bharat's plea to return, his
principles compelled.

No revenge, no malice, no anger did he bear,
As he bowed to Kaikeyi in Chitrakoot's air.
Humbly, he touched her feet in respect,
For her deeds, no bitterness did he project.

Redeemed Ahalya from a curse so grim,

Fought for Sugreeva and stood with him.
Jatayu's rites performed as his own,
Helping all who crossed his path unknown.

Savoured fruits bitten by Sabri's hand,
Hugged Guha, the boatman, across the land.
Hanuman found solace in his embrace,
For Shri Ram saw all as equals in grace.

Before Ravana fell to his final defeat,
He bade Lakshman to sit by his feet:
'Learn from the wise, their knowledge you
seek,
Even in battle, let's not let our ego creak.'

Shri Ram, the Maryada Purushottam divine,
Taught us virtues that forever shine–
Of forgiveness, humility and piety's light,
Timeless lessons to guide us right.

Krishna: The Eternal Guide

As Vishnu's Avatar, you graced the earth,
To guide us in love, compassion and mirth.
Your wisdom shines through the sacred Gita,
A beacon of truth, a cosmic mantra.

Your leelas enchant, your stories inspire,
Kindling devotion, setting hearts afire.
With Sudama, you showed that love has no
class,
A bond divine, no riches surpass.

You lifted Govardhan, a mountain grand,
To humble Indra with your steady hand.
Through Ras Leelas, you poured your
affection,
Teaching unity, love and connection.

Braving the venom of Nag Kaaliya's strife,
You danced on fear, restoring life.
Your teachings endure, a beacon of light,
Guiding our karma to paths that are right.

Focus on action; let outcomes release,
For in surrender lies ultimate peace.
Oh Krishna, eternal, your lessons impart,
A map to the soul, a song to the heart.

Shiva: The Cosmic Force

Shiva, the Mahadeva, supreme and wise,
An ascetic on Kailasa, beyond the skies.
Adiyogi, God of yoga and meditation,
Adorned with the crescent moon in divine
celebration.
With Ganga flowing through your hair,
A cosmic presence, beyond compare.

Your Tandav Nritya, a dance so wild,
An interplay of life and death compiled.
From Rudra Tandav, fierce and grand,

To Anand Tandav, joy on every hand.
Through your dance, the universe spins–
Creation, preservation, dissolution begin.

With ash on your body, third eye aglow,
You cleanse our sins and let us grow.
'Bhole Baba' – we call with heart so
pure,
In your grace, we find peace that endures.

With Parvati's Shakti, by your side,
You embody balance, the cosmic tide.
Together, you shape both build and destroy,
To bring harmony, peace and joy.

Shankara, Shambhu, Neelkantha, Rudra – so
many names,
Each utterance brings us closer, igniting the
flame.
Chanting your praises, we find divine light,
Guided by your power, day and night.

Guru Nanak: The Light of Unity

Ik Onkar, One God, eternal and true,
Unity and harmony in all we do.
Preaching equality, virtues to embrace,
A path of love, of truth and grace.

Guru Nanak sang Shabads, pure and bright,
In Japji Sahib, the song of light.
Teaching love for the divine so deep,
And how to find it in silence that we keep.

You showed the path to liberation's door,
Faith in divinity, our hearts to soar.
Ascetics and householders, you made clear,
That both paths lead to the same sphere.

As your immortal remains lay still,
Hindus and Muslims, with hearts full of will,
Fought for your rites, but as the sheet
unfurled,
Your body had turned to flowers, a sign for
the world.

You gave us the Nine Gurus, strong and wise,
To carry your message, to reach the skies.
To take Sikhism forward, spreading the word,
To unite all souls, where peace is heard.

Ik Onkar

One and only, the Infinite One,
The Supreme Power, where it all began.
One God, the source of all light,
Guiding creation through day and night.

Beyond time, beyond form,
The Eternal Spirit, the primal norm.
Unchanging, timeless, vast and whole,
The essence of life, the cosmic soul.

Bow to the One who governs all,
The source of rise, the reason for fall.
Creator of worlds, both seen and unseen,
Waheguru – the Truth, serene.

Kirat Karo

As life unfolds its trials and strife,
Remember the words that guide our life:
Guru Nanak's wisdom, timeless and true,
To earn with honesty in all that we do.

Through honest labour and pure intent,
Lies the path where blessings are sent.
A life well-lived, both just and fair,
Brings peace and joy beyond compare.

The skills and talents God imparts,
Are tools to serve with open hearts.
For self, for family, for all mankind,
Through rightful work, true purpose we find.

'Kirat Karo'—a noble way,
To live with honour every day.
In its embrace, there will be no dark night,
You will find a life of peace, serene and
bright.

Naam Japo – Path to Divine Grace

In the stillness of silence, softly abide,
Remember Akal Purkh, your Supreme guide.
He listens, His blessings flow,
Clearing the path, where obstacles grow.

With gratitude, reflect on all He provides,
Sing His praises; let joy reside.
For He shaped the world with infinite care,
A gift of love beyond compare.

Naam Japo to soothe the restless mind,
Naam Japo to leave all worries behind.
Naam Japo to see His beauty unfold,
Naam Japo to love Him, with devotion
untold.

Vand Chakko

This universe gives with an open heart,
No lines it draws, no lives set apart.
God made this world for all to share,
A gift of creation, beyond compare.

Let us learn from nature's way,
Its silent sharing, day by day.
A virtue so pure, we must embrace,
To build a world of love and grace.

Before a morsel touches your hand,
Look around – does someone else stand?
Dasvandh – ten percent to give,
A way to help all joyfully live.

Through Langars and the Saadh Sangat
divine,
Community thrives, hearts align.
Vand Chakko – for one and all,
Together we rise, together we call.

Buddha: The Path to Enlightenment

Buddha, the wandering ascetic, wise,
Spreading peace and unity, under endless
skies.
You left the kingdom and royal life,
To seek the truth, to end all strife.

You taught the Four Noble Truths to guide,
And the Noble Eightfold Path beside.
Mindfulness, kindness, Dhyana's grace,
You showed us how to find our place.

The 'Enlightened One', you touched the soul,
Turning Angulimaal from killer to whole.
From violence to peace, you paved the way,
A devout monk, to live and pray.

Your teachings transformed, from court to
shrine,
Courtesans to monks, a shift divine.
Your blessings gave Ananda peace of mind,
An ascetic life, of the highest kind.

Under the Bodhi tree, you sat in light,
A face aglow, your heart so bright.
Fully enlightened, you knew the way,
Through inclusion, not conquest, to lead the
day.

Four Noble Truths – Path to Liberation

Dukkha – the cycle of suffering profound,
What arises will fall, its grip all around.
Change and attachment, the roots of our
pain,
Sickness and death, sorrow they sustain.
Dukkha knows no end; its presence remains.

From Tanha – desire – the suffering flows,
Craving for more, where the discontent
grows.
A thirst for the new, to be what we're not,
A longing to escape what life has brought.

Yet Nirodha is within our reach,
Liberation from craving is what it will teach.
Freedom from longing, from clinging, from
ties,
Nirvana awaits where suffering dies.

The path to this truth, noble and wise,
The Eightfold Way, where enlightenment lies.
Right thought, right action and right speech
to start,
With mindfulness and Magga to guide the
heart.

The Noble Eightfold Path – Journey to Liberation

Samsara spins, a fleeting chain,
Its transient nature brings us pain.
But Buddha showed the Middle Way,
A path to peace, where joy will stay.

Right View to see the truth unfold,
The cause of pain in actions told.
Right Resolve to walk Dhamma's light,
With steadfast heart and inner might.

Right Speech, with words so kind and true,
Right Action, in all good we do.
Right Livelihood, with honest means,
A life of virtue, pure and clean.

Right Effort to cast off hatred's snare,
Right Mindfulness, with constant care.
Right Concentration, calm and deep,
A tranquil mind in wisdom steeped.

Follow this path, the Eightfold Way,
No pain or sorrow will cloud the day.
Liberation awaits, the soul set free,
From samsara's cycle, for eternity.

Karma

What you sow, you're destined to reap,
Each deed recorded, a ledger They keep.
Good or bad, all actions remain,
Their echoes felt through joy or pain.

Action alone is not the key,
Intent guides results we cannot see.
In this life or the next, they will unfold,
The story of karma, timelessly told.

Some karmas are fixed; their course is sealed,
While others are fluid, yet to be revealed.
Some bear fruit in the life you live,
For others, lessons rebirth give.

So tread with care, be mindful and wise,
For karma sees through all disguise.
Your actions, whether gentle or grim,
Will guide your soul back to Him.

Jesus: The Path of Love and Devotion

Incarnation of God, the awaited Messiah,
You brought love and compassion, lighting
the way.
Teaching the world, through your grace
divine,
The path to God, where hearts can pray.

You healed the sick with a touch so pure,
Walked on water, making hearts secure.
You resurrected the dead, bringing hope
anew,
Your miracles known to all who knew.

Risen from the dead, ascended above,
You washed away sins with boundless love.
You called us to devotion, a life set free,
To surrender ourselves and live for Thee.

The Light of Resurrection

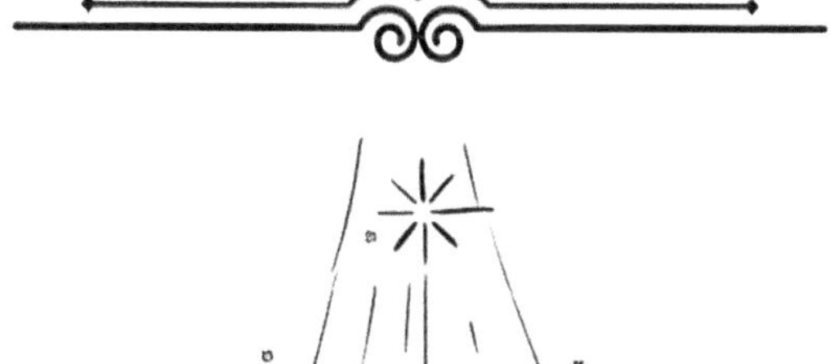

Resurrection – a sacred sign,
A promise of life, eternal, divine.
In death, a door to hope is shown,
Our future secure; we're never alone.

Jesus, the Son of God, arose,
From the grave, He conquered woes.
To give us faith, beyond the strife,
And assure us prayers breathe new life.

In the present, He offers His hand,
Guiding our steps to a promised land.
Through every trial, He walks beside,
A Saviour, our strength, our faithful guide.

So cast your worries into His care,
The Son of God is always there.
Rejoice this Easter, with hearts ablaze,
In happiness and dazzling praise.

The Glorious Ascension

The Son of God, from Heaven descended,
To walk among us, His love extended.
He then ascended, in the divine embrace,
He blesses His followers with endless grace.

From Earth's domain, John gazed above,
The cloud concealed the Lord he loved.
Faith proclaimed, as the heavens drew near,
Jesus ascended, alive and clear.

Forty days from the Resurrection's dawn,
To show His power, our fears withdrawn.
He healed our hearts; His promise stayed,
A guide in triumph, a light through the shade.

The Trinity

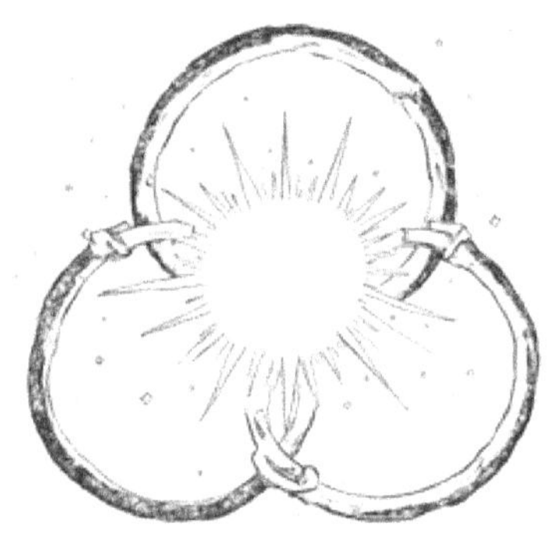

In the name of the Father, the Son and the
Holy Spirit,
Lies a truth eternal, for all to inherit.
The Shield of Trinity, a sacred sign,
Of equality, unity and love divine.

The Father – our Creator,
steadfast and true,
A parent's love in all that He'll do.
The universe made by His mighty hand,
Sending His Son as part of the plan.

The Son – God's Word in human
form,
Came to save us through life's storm.
With boundless love, He bore our pain,
Sacrificed Himself, so grace might reign.

The Holy Spirit – a gentle guide,
A dove of peace, forever by our side.
Empowering souls with gifts to share,
Teaching, sanctifying, with tender care.

The Trinity shines, three yet one,
Father, Spirit and the Son.
A holy mystery, pure and blessed,
In their embrace, we find our rest

Consciousness

Eternal, divine – unchanged by time,
Unburned by flame, uncut by blade,
Unwet by waters' endless flow,
A truth within us, ever-glade.

It transcends the years, the centuries,
A light that guides, a soul's embrace.
Those who awaken to its call,
Dance in joy, in boundless grace.

The fleeting world fades to a blur,
As they connect with what is whole.
No borders bind, no walls divide,
Consciousness speaks to every soul.

One Humanity, One Love

Let there be no religion,
For all faiths are one,
Each teaching us to harm none,
And love all, under the sun.

Humanity should be our creed,
Let every human be our God,
The world our sacred place indeed,
Serving all is our prayer, unflawed.

Be it Shyam, Raminder or Ramine,
It is in service that we find the divine.
Be it Ram, Nanak or Christ,
To bow in love is the holiest rite.

Let there be no world of blood,
Where children sleep, starving in the night,
Where women lack wings to fly above,
Where men cross borders, waging fight.

Let there be only love,
Let there be only care,
Let there be only sharing,
Let there be only peace everywhere.

No religion teaches hatred,
No faith leads to devastation,
All are deserving of celebration,
For we are all illuminated in creation.